ALEXA,

THINKING OF YO...

AND YOUR UNFINISHED GARDEN!

L. D

Invitation to Kyoto Gardens

京都の名園

Photographs by Kenzo Yamamoto

SUIKO BOOKS

■CONTENTS (The Location of Gardens and Transportation Guide)

27 Kōetsu-ji	Takagamine Kita Takagamine-cho 47, Kita-ku	From Shijo-omiya take the #6 Municipal bus and get off at Takagamine Genkō-an mae.
28 Kinkaku-ji	Kinkaku-ji-cho 1, Kita-ku	Take the #101 or #204 or #205 Municipal bus and get off at Kinkaku-ji Michi.
29 Ryōan-ji	Ryoan-ji Goryo Shitamachi 13, Ukyo-ku	Take the #59 or special(toku)#59 and get off at Ryoan-ji Michi.
30 Ninna-ji	Omuro Ouchi 33, Ukyo-ku	Take the #26 Municipal bus and get off at Omuro Ninna-ji mae.
31 Tōji-in	Toji-in Kitamachi 63, Kita-ku	Take the #50 Municipal bus and get off at Hakubai-cho.
32 Taizō-in	Hanazono Myōshin-ji-cho 35, Ukyo-ku	Take the #26 Municipal bus and get off at Myoshin-ji Kitamom mae.
33 Keishun-in	Hanazono Terano Naka-cho 11, Ukyo-ku	Take the #26 Municipal bus and get off at Myōshin-ji Kitamon mae.
34 Hōkongō-in	Hanazono Ogino-cho 49, Ukyo-ku	Take the JR San'in Line and get off at Hanazono Station.
35 Ōsawa Pond	Saga Osawa-cho 4, Ukyo-ku	Take the #28 Municipal bus and get off at Daikaku-ji mae.
36 Giō-ji	Saga Torii Motokosaka-cho 32, Ukyo-ku	Take the #72 Kyoto bus and get off at Sagashaka-do mae.
37 Tenryū-ji	Saga Tenryu-ji Susukino Baba-cho 68, Ukyo-ku	Take the JR San'in Line and get off at Saga-arashiyama Station.
38 Rokuō-in	Saga Kita Hori-cho 24, Ukyo-ku	Take the JR San'in Line and get off at Saga-arashiyama Station.
39 Umenomiya Taisha(Shrine)	Umezu Fukeno-cho 30, Ukyo-ku	Take the #28 or #71 Municipal bus and get off at Umenomiya-jinja mae,
40 Jizō-in	Yamada Kitano-cho 23, Nishikyo-ku	Take the Hankyu Line and get off at Kamikatsura Station.
41 Katsura Imperial Villa	Katsura Shimizu-cho, Nishikyo-ku	Take the #33 Municipal bus and get off at Katsura Rikyu mae.
42 Byōdō-in	Uji Renge 116, Uji-shi	Take the JR Nara Line and get off at Uji Station.
43 Kajū-ji	Kanshu-ji Niodo-cho 27-6, Yamashina-ku	Take the Municipal Tozai Subway Line to Ono Station.
44 Zuishin-in	Ono Goryo-cho 35, Yamashina-ku	Take the Municipal Tozai Subway Line to Ono Station.
45 Jōnan-gū(Shrine)	Nakajima Tobarikyu-cho 7, Fushimi-ku	From the Kintetsu Kyoto Line Takeda Station take the south (minami)#1 or south(minami)#2 Municipal bus and get off at Jonan-gu Higashi-guchi.
46 Shūon-an	Takigi Sato no Uchi 102, Kyotanabe-shi	Take the Kintetsu Line from Kyoto Station and get off at Shin Tanabe Station.
47 Jōruri-ji	Oaza Nishi Koaza Satsuba 40, Kamo-cho, Soraku-gun	From JR Nara Station take the Nara Kotsu bus bound for Jōruri-ji, get off at Jōruri-ji.

The above directions on transportation begin from Kyoto Station

Invitation to Kyoto Gardens

First Edition April 1989
First Revised Edition May 2001 by Mitsumura Suiko Shoin Co.,Ltd.
Kitayama-dori Horikawa higashi-iru Kita-ku, Kyoto 603-8115 Japan

Photographs : Kenzo Yamamoto
English Translation : Tom Wright
Editor : Yasuhiro Asano
Editorial Coordinator : Michiko Takagi
Publisher : Kozo Nagasawa

©2001 Kenzo Yamamoto   Printed in Japan

ISBN4-8381-0101-5

京都の名園
Invitation to Kyoto Gardens

山本 建三
Kenzo Yamamoto

光村推古書院

1. 京都御所小御所御池庭
江戸時代　池泉廻遊
紫宸殿の東北にある小御所の前庭。
粒のそろった栗石を敷きつめた美し
い浜がひろがるおおらかな庭。

1. Kyoto Imperial Palace
Edo period; stroll garden with pond
This is the front garden of the Minor
Palace located to the northeast of the
Shishinden. The dark flat "chestnut"
stones as they are called, are beauti-
fully laid out, creating a most serene
and settled shore.

2. 仙洞御所南庭
江戸時代　池泉廻遊
北池と南池を中心にひろがる大庭園。
対岸に見える醍花亭茶室の前に、石浜
がやわらかな曲線を描いている。

2. Sentō Imperial Palace
Edo period; stroll garden with pond
This large garden centers around a
north and south pond. On the opposite
bank, in front of the teahouse Sei-
katei, one can observe the soft curve
of the rocky shore.

3．二条城二の丸庭園
桃山時代　池泉廻遊
将軍上洛時の居館として，慶長年間
に造営された。中島及び護岸の石組
等豪華を極め,桃山を代表する庭園。

3. Nijō Castle
Momoyama period; stroll garden with pond
The Ninomaru structure was built for
Tokugawa Ieyasu, and completed in
1603. The garden contains a pond and
an unusually gorgeous display of
stone grouping prominent during the
previous Momoyama period.

４．大仙院方丈東北庭
室町時代　枯山水
大徳寺塔頭。山水画を見るような枯
滝から清流は巨石の間をぬい，自然
石の橋をくぐって大河の様相を表す。

4. Daisen-in
Muromachi period; *kare sansui* or dry
landscape garden
Simulating a grand landscape (though
actually only 118 sq. meters), clear
water seems to fall from this dry
waterfall, wending its way through
huge boulders, and dipping under a
natural stone bridge into the ocean.

5. 龍源院方丈南庭
昭和　枯山水
一枝坦とよばれる庭。中央に石組を配し蓬莱山を表す。写真は左方にある亀島で、丸い苔山が独創性を持つ。

5. Ryōgen-in
Showa period; dry landscape garden
Referred to as the Isshidan Garden, the rock setting in the middle of the garden depicts Mt. Horai. The rock on the left depicts a *tortoise island*, a symbol of longevity, while the circular mound of moss symbolizes independence.

6．瑞峯院方丈前庭
昭和　枯山水
白砂に砂紋を描いて波を表し，苔で
築山を盛り，巨石を組んで須弥山と
なし，天地自然を造形化している。

6. Zuihō-in
Showa period; dry landscape garden
The raked white sand looks like
waves; with the moss built up, the
large stoneworks depict Mt. Sumeru,
in Buddhist cosmology, the highest
mountain which rises out of the vast
ocean. This is a model of heaven and
earth-the universe.

7. 銀閣寺（慈照寺）庭園
室町時代　池泉廻遊
端正な砂紋の銀沙灘と，円錐状に盛
り上げた向月台が，背景の緑や銀閣
と鮮やかな景観をなしている。

7. Ginkaku-ji
Muromachi period; stroll garden with pond
The Ginsadan or "Sea of Silver Sand" and the shaved conical white sand mountain, Kogetsudai, form a spectacular backdrop from which to enjoy the panoply of greens and the Silver Pavilion itself.

8. 白沙村荘庭園
昭和　池泉廻遊
日本画壇の巨匠，橋本関雪が自ら構成した庭。全国から集めた石仏・石塔が竹林の間に点在し，趣がある。

8. Hakusason-so
Showa period; stroll garden with pond
This garden is the product of Hashimoto Kansetsu, a luminary figure in the Japanese art world. Scattered throughout the bamboo grove are a collection of very fine stone buddhas and gravestones.

9．法然院庭園
江戸時代　池泉廻遊

鹿ヶ谷善気山の麓にある閑静な寺。
法然上人の開創に始まる。侘びた茅
葺きの山門から見た砂壇が印象的。

9. Hōnen-in
Edo period; stroll garden with pond

A quiet secluded temple at the foot of
Zenkizan in Shishigatani. Hōnen-in
was founded by Saint Hōnen (1133
~1212). Viewed from the simple yet
elegant thatch-roofed gate, the sand
mounds on either side of the walkway
are very impressive.

10. 平安神宮中神苑
明治　池泉廻遊
蒼龍池を中心とした中神苑は，池に
珊瑚島があって三条・五条大橋の橋
柱を利用した沢飛石が打たれている。

10. Heian Jingū (Shrine)
Meiji period; stroll garden with pond
Soryu Pond forms the centerpiece of
this garden. In the middle of the pond
there is a small coral island. The
stepping stones laid out came from
the pillars of the old Sanjo and Gojo
bridges.

11. 南禅寺方丈庭園
江戸時代　枯山水
東南隅に最も大きな石を据え，西へ
次第に低く石組と刈込を配している。
白砂を前景とした禅院式枯山水。

11. Nanzen-ji
Edo period; dry landscape garden
Westward from the large rock set in
the southeast corner, the rocks
decrease in size and a varied arrangement of shrubbery come into view.
The foreground of white sand is representative of the Zen dry landscape
garden style.

12. 天授庵庭園
南北朝時代　枯山水
方丈に至る延段は，正方形と菱形に
置いた角石を細長い切石で縁取り，
砂紋や苔と見事に調和している。

12. Tenju-an
Nanbokucho period; dry landscape garden
The walkway extending to the abbot's quarter's is itself squared with stones set in a square and diamond pattern. Along the edges, rather thin rectangularly cut stones have been laid. The white sand and emerald green moss lend a harmonious touch to this garden.

13. 金地院庭園
江戸時代　枯山水
鶴亀式庭園の代表的傑作で，豪壮な
石組・刈込等がひときわ印象的。遠
州が設計，庭師賢庭が作庭した。

13. Konchi-in
Edo period; dry landscape garden
A magnificent representative of the
tortoise-crane style, the gorgeous
stoneworks and shrubbery are especially lovely. This garden was designed
by the master gardener Kobori Enshu
and put together by gardener Kentei.

14. 無鄰菴庭園
明治　池泉廻遊
東山を借景とし，琵琶湖疏水を引い
て東部に三段落の滝口を組み，多く
の常緑樹を植えている奥深い庭。

14. Murin-an
Meiji period; stroll garden with pond
Borrowing the hills of the Higashi-
yama for a backdrop, this very
exquisite garden draws water by way
of *sosui*, or canal, coming from
Lake Biwa. On the eastern side, a
three-tiered waterfall has been laid
out; the luxuriant evergreens give
added depth to the garden.

15. 青蓮院庭園
江戸時代　池泉廻遊
小御所から好文亭へと細長く伸びた
龍心池には孤形の石橋や滝口が組ま
れ，楓や萩が風趣を添えている。

15. Shōren-in
Edo period; stroll garden with pond
Ryushin Pond, "Pond of the Dragon's
Heart," runs from the Kogosho (or
Minor Palace) to the Kobuntei. A
crescent shaped bridge with the crest of
a waterfall having been built into the
design; sugar maples and hagi (bush
clover) add special charm.

16. 高台寺庭園
江戸時代　池泉廻遊
東山を借景として，仏殿から開山堂へと廊橋が架かり東の臥龍池，西の偃月池に分かれている。

16. Kōdai-ji
Edo period; stroll garden with pond
Borrowing the hills of the Higashi-yama for a backdrop, a bridge-like walkway extends from the Butsuden or Buddha Hall to the Kaisando; on the east side lies Garyu Pond and on the west side, Engetsu Pond.

17. 智積院庭園
江戸時代　池泉観賞
池水は，書院の床下にも流れ込み，
泉殿のような様式となっている。水
墨画のような景観の庭である。

17. Chishaku-in
Edo period; pond viewing garden
The pond extending under the veranda
of the *shoin* gives an *izumidono* affect,
that is, a feeling that the building had
been built over a spring. This is also a
good vantage point from which to
appreciate the garden. The azaleas
blooming in April and May are an
added bonus.

18. 東福寺方丈北庭
昭和　枯山水
北庭は苔と石による市松模様が構成
される。主庭の南庭は鋭い巨石を中
心に，神仙島をかたどっている。

18. Tōfuku-ji
Showa period; dry landscape garden
The north garden is a checkerboard
pattern called *ichimatsu moyo*, while the
main garden, the south garden,
centers around several jagged rocks.
This one was modeled after an island
of mythical religious hermits.

19. 芬陀院方丈南庭
室町時代　枯山水
雪舟の作といわれている庭。二重基
段の亀島に，剛健な亀頭石が屹立し
ている。鶴島は折鶴を表現する。

19. Funda-in
Muromachi period; dry landscape garden
This garden is attributed to Sesshu.
The tortoise island is arranged in two
layers with the head of the tortoise
thrusting its noble head toward the
heavens; the crane island motif is an
expression of the folded paper crane,
popular in Japanese origami.

20. 三千院有清園
江戸時代　池泉廻遊
優雅な阿弥陀三尊をまつる往生極楽
院の背景にある，侘びた古建築と調
和する幽玄な庭。

20. Sanzen-in
Edo period; stroll garden with pond
This garden is located behind Ojo-
gokurakuin where an elegant Amida
Buddha and two bodhisattva escorts
are enshrined. The old architecture
blends harmoniously with the quiet
beauty of the garden.

21. 蓮華寺庭園
江戸時代　池泉観賞
高野川の水を引いた池泉庭園。豊潤
な池は書院の前に広がり，鶴島・亀
島を配している。

21. Renge-ji
Edo period; pond viewing garden
This stroll garden with a pond draws
water from the Takano River. In front
of the *shoin* there is a pond looking
refreshingly cool with tortoise and
crane islands.

22. 修学院離宮上の御茶屋庭園
江戸時代　池泉廻遊
上の御茶屋庭園から浴龍池を望んだ
景観。背景の岩倉や鞍馬の山並を借
景とし、比類のない壮大さを示す。

22. Shūgaku-in Imperial Villa
Edo period; stroll garden with pond
A splendid view of Yokuryu Pond can
be seen from the *Kami no Chaya*, or
Upper Area. With the hills of Iwakura
and Kurama in the background, one
takes in a view of incomparable
grandeur.

23. 曼殊院庭園
江戸時代　枯山水
遠州好みの枯山水庭園。枯流れは芝
生・植栽をめぐり白砂によって洋々
たる水を表している。

23. Manshu-in
Edo period; dry landscape garden
This *kare sansui* or dry landscape
garden is in the Kobori Enshu style.
Swirling around the mossy carpets of
green and variegated trees and
hedges, the river of white sand gives
rise to feelings of boundless expanse.

24. 詩仙堂庭園
江戸時代　枯山水
やわらかな半円形のサツキ，ツツジ
の刈込の前に，豊かに白砂が展開す
る。添水の音が冴えた音をたてる。

24. Shisen-dō
Edo period; dry landscape garden
The soft curves of the clipped azaleas
harmonize with the river of white
sand. A *sozu* or bamboo device that
fills with water and then drops with a
sharp crack was formerly used to
scare away deer.

25. 金福寺庭園
江戸時代　枯山水
白砂の庭を埋めるが如くツツジの刈
込が重なりあい，その背後に芭蕉が
寓居した草庵の屋根が見える。

25. Konpuku-ji
Edo period; dry landscape garden
The garden of white sand seems to
become almost buried in the layer
upon layer of surrounding azaleas. In
the background stands a cottage
where the poet Basho lived in tem-
porarily.

26. 正伝寺方丈東庭
江戸時代　枯山水
比叡山を借景にし，東を築地塀で仕
切り，白砂を敷き右から七五三の石
組にツツジなどの刈込を配している。

26. Shōden-ji
Edo period; dry landscape garden
The low whitewashed wall delineates
the borrowed scenery of Mt. Hiei
from the river of white sand in the
foreground. The rounded boulders of
green clipped azaleas are arranged in
the traditionally lucky order of seven
five three.

27. 光悦寺太虚庵
江戸時代　枯山水
本阿弥光悦が晩年を過ごした太虚庵の遺跡。光悦垣，又は臥牛垣とよばれる斬新なデザインの竹垣が有名。

27. Kōetsu-ji
Edo period; dry landscape garden
Hon'ami Koetsu spent his final years at Taikoan. Today only the remains of Taikoan cottage are left as testimony of Hon'ami's residence during his last years. This garden with its lovely maples is famous for the *Kōetsugaki (Gagyugaki)*, original designs for woven bamboo fences.

28. 金閣寺（鹿苑寺）庭園
鎌倉時代　池泉廻遊
鏡湖池畔の有名な金閣は，1987年に
その金箔が貼りかえられ，黄金色に
眩しく輝き人気をよんでいる。

28. Kinkaku-ji
Kamakura period; stroll garden with pond
The world famous Kinkaku Pavilion,
poised at the edge of *Kyokoike* or
"Mirror Pond," was regilded with
gold leaf in 1987. In rain, snow, or
sunshine, a walk around this garden is
an unforgettable experience.

29. 龍安寺方丈庭園
室町時代　枯山水
白砂を敷き詰めた庭上に15個の石が
配置され, 砂紋をくっきりと際立さ
せている庭園は, 石庭を代表する。

29.Ryōan-ji
Muromachi period; dry landscape garden
The crisp lines of the waves of sand
accentuate the fifteen rocks (though
all 15 are not visible from any one
angle except by the enlightened eye)
carefully laid out on the bed of white
sand; thought by many to be the best
representative of the rock garden
style of *kare sansui*.

30. 仁和寺庭園
江戸時代　池泉廻遊
宸殿の北に造られたこの庭園は，前面に白砂を置いて，屈曲した池とその向こうに築山を配している。

30. Ninna-ji
Edo period; stroll garden with pond
This garden, constructed on the north side of the *shinden*, is comprised of white sand in the front portion forming a softly winding shore along the edge of the pond, while the other side has been arranged with *tsukiyama*, taking advantage of the natural slope.

31. 等持院方丈北庭
江戸時代　池泉廻遊
書院対岸に武家風茶室の清漣亭が見
える。芙蓉池の流れは，石橋をくぐ
り東庭の心字池へと続いている。

31. Tōji-in
Edo period; stroll garden with pond
Across the pond from the *shoin*
stands a teahouse, Seirentei, built in
the ruling family style. Water from
Fuyo Pond flows around a stone
bridge into Shinji Pond in the eastern
garden.

亀島

32. 退蔵院方丈西庭
室町時代　枯山水
狩野元信の作と伝えられる庭。枯池
を穿ち、中央に蓬莱島を設けて，多
数の庭石を豪快に組んでいる。

32. Taizō-in
Muromachi period; dry landscape garden
This garden is said to have been
designed by Kano Motonobu. *Horaijima*
rises sharply out of the old pond.
Numerous rocks have been laid out
beautifully in this semi stroll garden.

33. 桂春院方丈東庭
江戸時代　枯山水
思惟の庭とも呼ばれる。方丈東側の
左右の築山に十六羅漢石、中央に座
禅石を配した幽邃閑雅な枯山水。

33. Keishun-in
Edo period; dry landscape garden
This garden is also called the "Meditation Garden." On either side of the *tsukiyama* on the eastern side of the abbot's residence, there stand sixteen *arhat* saints. In the center, there is a meditation rock for sitting zazen – a truly serene and quiet garden.

34. 法金剛院庭園
平安時代　池泉廻遊
1970年に発掘復元された庭。青女の
滝と呼ばれる石組は，創建当初の遺
構をそのままに残している。

34. Hōkongō-in
Heian period; stroll garden with pond
This garden was excavated and
restored in 1970. Seinyo no Taki or
"Waterfall of the Virgin" has been
left just as it was from the estab-
lishment of the garden.

35. 大沢池（大覚寺）
平安時代　池泉舟遊
嵯峨御所と呼ばれた大覚寺に隣する
大沢池は，北嵯峨随一の景勝地で，
現存する京都最古の庭園である。

35. Ōsawa Pond at Daikaku-ji
Heian period; *chisen shuyu* or both
garden and pond viewed from a boat
Ōsawa Pond lies next to Daikaku-ji,
often referred to as the Saga Palace.
The garden is the oldest in existence in
Kyoto, and certainly ranks as one of
the finest views in the North Saga
area.

36. 祇王寺庭園
明治　露地
『平家物語』で知られる祇王と仏御前の悲話の舞台となった寺。しみじみと奥嵯峨の情緒を語ってくれる。

36. Giō-ji
Meiji period; *roji* or pathway and garden to the teahouse
Giō-ji is the setting for the tragic tale between Gio and Hotoke Gozen in the Tales of Heike. This garden most impressively reveals the powerful passion and emotion buried deeply in Saga.

37. 天龍寺庭園
鎌倉時代　池泉廻遊
曹源池を中心とする庭は，嵐山を借景とし，州浜の曲線の美しさや，緊密な構成の滝石組など見所が多い。

37. Tenryū-ji
Kamakura period; stroll garden with pond
This pond garden for strolling and viewing from the veranda centers around Sogen Pond, borrowing the hills of Arashiyama for a backdrop. The beauty of the curves of the sandy beach, the tightly knit composition of the stonework waterfall are among many splendid features of the garden.

38. 鹿王院庭園
江戸時代　枯山水
閑静な境内の中で，沙羅双樹が青苔
の上に散る姿は，初夏の嵐山の風物
詩となるほど興趣つきない。

38. Rokuō-in
Edo period; dry landscape garden
Inside the serenity of the compound
one never tires of the scene of the
flowers of the sal tree falling on the
mossy carpet; the natural poetry of
Arashiyama in early summer.

39. 梅宮大社神苑
江戸時代　池泉廻遊

さくや池を中心とする神苑は，花菖蒲やかきつばたが咲く初夏が美しい。島には茶室の芦のまろやがある。

39. Umenomiya Taisha (Shrine)
Edo period; stroll garden with pond

A pond is the centerpiece of this garden along with the surrounding fence. The sweet flag and rabbit ear irises are remarkably stunning in early summer. On the island stands a teahouse called *Ashi no Maroya*.

40. 地蔵院方丈前庭
室町時代　枯山水
点在する石は，修行する十六羅漢の
姿を表している。平庭式のこの庭は，
青い苔と刈込も美しい。

40. Jizō-in
Muromachi period; dry landscape garden
The rocks dotting the garden represent sixteen arhats (Buddhist saints)
deep in their training. A *hiraniwa*, or
flat garden, the emerald green moss,
and the trimmed shrubbery are
particularly beautiful.

41. 桂離宮松琴亭庭園
桃山時代　池泉廻遊
形のよい石庭で二つの島をつなぎ、松を配して天の橋立を象徴する。岬の先端に燈籠をあしらっている。

41. Katsura Imperial Villa
Momoyama period; stroll garden with pond
An elegantly curved stone bridge joins two islands. The arrangement of pines suggests Ama no Hashidate, one of the three most beautiful sites in Japan. At the tip of the promontory stands a single stone lantern.

42. 平等院鳳凰堂庭園
平安時代　池泉廻遊
鳳凰堂前の阿字池は、ゆるやかな曲
汀を描き平安期の原型をとどめる。
極楽浄土を表現した浄土式庭園。

42. Byōdō-in
Heian period; stroll garden with pond
The soft lines of the shoreline of
Ajiike Pond in front of the Phoenix
Hall are of a pattern limited to the
Heian period. The garden is an
expression of the Western Paradise of
the Jōdo school of Buddhism.

43. 勧修寺庭園
平安時代　池泉舟遊
水戸黄門が寄進したといわれる燈籠
が有名。氷室池には，初夏に睡蓮や
花菖蒲が一面に咲きみだれる。

43. Kanshū-ji
Heian period; *chisen shuyu* or both
garden and pond viewed from a boat.
The garden is famous for a stone
lantern said to have been donated by
Mito Kōmon. The water lilies and
rabbit ear irises in Himuro Pond
bloom in splendid fashion in early
summer.

44. 随心院庭園
江戸時代　池泉廻遊
四季を通して美しい庭。特に春には，
石楠花や霧島ツツジが咲き誇る。梅
雨の頃の苔のつややかさも見どころ。

44. Zuishin-in
Edo period; stroll garden with pond
This garden is beautiful throughout
the four seasons, but particularly
during the spring when the shakunage
(rhododendron) and the kirishima
azaleas are in bloom. The luminosity
of the moss in the rainy season is
unforgettable.

45. 城南宮神苑
昭和　池泉廻遊　枯山水
茶亭楽水軒を中心に北側に池泉庭園
が，南には豪快な枯山水庭園がひろ
がる。苔と桜との対照が美しい。

45. Jōnan-gū (Shrine)
Showa period; stroll garden with pond
The north garden, a Muromachi
Momoyama period style stroll garden, centers around Rakusuiken, a
teahouse. The south garden is a
breathtaking dry landscape style *kare
sansui*. The green emerald of the
moss contrasts beautifully with the
blooming cherry trees in spring.

46. 酬恩庵方丈北庭
江戸時代　枯山水
北庭の東北隅には雄渾な石組が展開
する。巨大な観音石を中心に，深山
幽谷を表す。枯山水の傑作といえる。

46. Shūon-an
Edo period; dry landscape garden
In the northeast corner of the garden
stand some extremely bold stonework. Centering around an imposing
rock called *Kannonseki*, the stonework is an expression of deep mountains and dark valleys. It is a master-
piece in the dry landscape style.

47. 浄瑠璃寺庭園
平安時代　池泉廻遊
阿字池に美しい甍を映す本堂には、
九体の阿弥陀如来が祀られている。
浄土の仏世界を表現する庭である。

47. Jōruri-ji
Heian period; stroll garden with pond
With an *Ajiike Pond* reflecting the
roof tiles of the *hondo* (sanctuary),
there are also enshrined nine Amida
Nyorai in various postures. The garden is an expression of Amida Buddha's pureland world according to the
teachings of the Jōdo school.

京都の名園

Invitation to Kyoto Gardens

Commentary and Information Guide
Garden and Other Terms
Historical Periods and Prominent Garden Styles
Application to see the Kyoto Imperial Palaces and the Imperial Villas
Map of Kyoto Gardens

The visitor's fees listed here are as of April 1, 2001

■ Commentary and Information Guide

1. Kyoto Imperial Palace

The gardens within the palace grounds include the south garden of white sand in front of the Shishinden, in addition to the garden in front of the Seiryoden. The views of the Oike Garden from either Gogakumonsho or Otsunegoten have been well considered, reflecting a style of imperial artistic technique.

◆Permission is needed. Application should be made at the Imperial Household Agency. If there is room in the tour group on the day application is made, it may be possible to make application and be allowed entry on the same day. (Refer to page 62)

2. Sentō Imperial Palace

The Tokugawa Shogunate decided to construct the Sentō Palace for retired Emperor Gomizuno, in the fifth year of Kan'ei, 1628. Master gardener, Kobori Enshu was appointed *bugyo* or supervisor for carrying out the actual construction. The garden is divided into three parts; *shin, gyo,* and *so,* and each displays its own charm with grace and refinement.

◆Permission is needed. Application should be made at the Imperial Household Agency. If there is room in the tour group on the day application is made, it may be possible to make application and be allowed entry on the same day. (Refer to page 62) There are no tours conducted in English.

3. Nijō Castle

The Ninomaru Garden is said to have been constructed by Kobori Enshu in 1624, prior to his assignment to the Sentō Imperial Palace. The huge stone bridge leading to the central stonework of the pond, Horaijima, along with the overall composition of imposing stonework, blend skillfully with the gorgeous *shoin*.

◆Visitor's fee: ¥600.   Open: 8:45~16:00

4. Daisen-in

Kogaku Sotan Zenji founded Daisen-in shortly after the end of the Onin War (1467~1477) which beckoned the beginning of the decline of Ashikaga rule. This *Sekitei*, or rock garden, lies to the northeast of the *hojo* or abbot's quarters. Within the con-

fines of a very narrow space enclosed by an earthen wall, the garden employs very bold stonework. Sotan himself is said to have constructed the garden.

◆Visitor's fee: ¥400.   Open: 9:00~17:00

5. Ryōgen-in

The photograph is of the south garden of the *hojo* at Ryōgen-in. The *hojo* is surrounded on all sides by gardens. The north garden, Ryugin-an, is of the *kare sansui* style and contains a trio of stones called the *sanson iwagumi,* or sacred trinity, unique to Muromachi period gardens. This *sanson* trio symbolizes Mt. Sumeru of Buddhist mythology. On the east side of the *hojo* is a tiny *tsubo niwa* called Totekiko, and symbolizes the limitless waves created by one drop of water which has fallen into the great ocean of the universe.

◆Visitor's fee: ¥350.   Open: 9:00~16:30 (Closed until may 2002)

6. Zuihō-in

The photograph is of the front garden of the *hojo* at Zuihō-in. This garden was an offering to the Buddha and constructed by Shigemori Mirei in 1961. The front garden called Dokuza no Niwa takes its theme from the name of the temple Zuihō meaning the great ocean and steep mountains. Behind the *hojo* is another garden, Kanmin no Niwa, or Garden of Tranquility.

◆Visitor's fee: ¥400.   Open: 9:00~16:30

7. Ginkaku-ji

This garden is comprised of the areas in front of the Tōgudo and in front of the Ginkaku or Silver Pavilion itself, with Kinkyo Pond as the centerpiece. The two areas of the garden are connected by a natural stone bridge called Ryuhaikyo, or Dragon's Back. The walkway leading up to the garden area is enclosed on both sides by very high immaculately clipped camelia hedges making it very impressive. Though Ginkaku-ji means Silver Temple, it was never covered by silver leaf in the way its counterpart across town (the Golden Pavilion) was.

◆Visitor's fee: ¥500.   Open: 8:30~17:00 (9:00~16:30, Dec. 1-March 14)

8. Hakusason-so

Hashimoto Kansetsu poured all his energy into making this

garden, the perfect retirement place for a man of great letters who was both unique and original in style. In the middle of the garden, there is a large pond that sweeps around; off to the side there's a simple, quiet teahouse. The kansetsu cherry trees along the stream in front of the Hakusason-so are gorgeous.

◆Visitor's fee: ¥800.   Open: 10:00~17:00

9. Hōnen-in

Water, a symbol of purity, is present concretely in the pond and abstractly through the raked waves on the sand mounds flanking the walkway. On an island in the middle of the pond are three *sansonseki*, Amida Buddha and his entourage, representing crossing over to the Western Paradise. Honen-in is particularly famous for its camelia in early spring.

◆No charge for garden viewing.   Open: 6:00~16:00

10. Heian Jingū (Shrine)

This shrine was built in 1895 and dedicated to Emperors Kanmu and Komei, founders of the city of Kyoto, then called Miyako. The garden is divided into a western, central, and eastern portion. All were arranged by Ogawa Jihei. The blue flag irises in the central garden pictured in this book are especially lovely.

◆Visitor's fee: ¥600.   Open: 8:30~17:30

11. Nanzen-ji

Constructed at the end of the Kamakura period, originally, this temple served as a villa for Emperor Kameyama. During the succeeding Muromachi period, Nanzen-ji was designated as one of the *gozan*, or Five Major Monasteries. (The *gozan* are supported by the imperial family). It houses many famous ink paintings. The greater *hojo* is the former Seiryoden which was donated by the imperial family. The garden unfolds on the south side. The large sliding doors in the *hojo* are famous for their tiger and her cubs motif.

◆Visitor's fee: ¥400.   Open: 8:40~17:00

12. Tenju-an

The garden was originally constructed during the Nanbokucho period (1336~1392), but was redone during the Meiji period (1868~1912). The pond is divided by two peninsulas creating an east and west section. The design of the garden exhibits the classic characteristics of the Nanbokucho period garden when the country was divided into the southern and northern dynasties. Stonework, including a waterfall, connect the east and west ponds.

◆Visitor's fee: ¥300.   Open: 9:00~17:00

13. Konchi-in

The front portion of the garden is laid with white sand representing the ocean. Behind this on either side are *tortoise-crane* stoneworks, the crane seemingly lifting off in flight. Between these is a large horizontally flat worship stone from which reverence can be paid to the Toshogu, a shrine dedicated to Tokugawa Ieyasu. In the background, there is a stonework depicting Mt. Horai, mythical dwelling place of many religious saints, as well as layer upon layer of well trimmed shrubbery representing deep mountains and hidden valleys.

◆Visitor's fee: ¥400.   Open: 8:30~17:00 (open until 16:30 in winter)

14. Murin-an

Yamagata Aritomo, a Meiji period statesman, designed the garden for his villa and commissioned Ogawa Jihei to do the actual construction. Containing a three-tiered waterfall and two separate streams, this garden has a light and natural feeling to it.

◆Visitor's fee: ¥350.   Open: 9:00~16:30

15. Shōren-in

Traditionally, this temple belonged to the Tendai school of Buddhism. From the northern edge of the pond and moving toward a teahouse Kobuntei, in a variegated scenery of greenery Kirishima no Niwa azaleas, golden yellow kerria, asebi or Japanese andromeda — all dot the landscape. There is also a palanquin shaped stone lantern offered by Toyotomi Hideyoshi. Outside the temple along the slope leading up to the gate are three huge camphor trees of unforgettable size and shape.

◆Visitor's fee: ¥500.   Open: 9:00~17:00

16. Kōdai-ji

Hideyoshi's wife of the Kita-no-mandokoro (he had several wives) had the temple built, and installed Sanko Osho, former abbot of Kennin-ji, as the founder. The ancestral mausoleum and the Kaisando or Founder's Memorial Hall still stand from the Momoyama period. The view with Ryozen in the background as *borrowed scenery* is magnificent.

◆Visitor's fee: ¥500.　Open: 9:00~17:00

17. Chishaku-in

Utilizing the natural incline on the east side of the *shoin*, rocks and shrubbery have been arranged to create the feeling of layer upon layer of high mountains. In the center of the garden, a dry waterfall has been set up over which extends a narrow stone bridge. At the foot is a pond exemplifying the Yangtze River in China.

◆Visitor's fee: ¥350.　Open: 9:00~16:00

18. Tōfuku-ji

The photograph is of the north garden of the *hojo* at Tōfuku-ji. The garden in the *honbo-hojo* (north side) was constructed by Shigemori Mirei during the Showa period. The Hasso Garden, or Garden of Eight Faces, is famous because of the changes in the garden when viewing it from different angles.

◆Visitor's fee: ¥400.(for the Hondo and Kaizan Hall)　Open: 9:00~16:00

19. Funda-in

The photograph is of the south garden of the *hojo* at Funda-in. This is a sub-temple within the Tōfuku-ji complex; it is also referred to as Sesshu-dera, since the famous landscape painter Sesshu is said to have stayed there when visiting Kyoto. Besides the south garden, the view out of the round window at the *hojo* onto the east garden is set in a framework from which to appreciate the elegant charm of this garden. The crane island motif is the centerpiece of the east garden, depicting Mt. Horai. Along with that of the south garden, the moss of this dry landscape garden is superb.

◆Visitor's fee: ¥300.　Open: 9:0~17:00

20. Sanzen-in

There is a *tsuru kame* or crane and tortoise motif in the middle of the pond running north and south which interlaces with the

shore. Sanzen-in in the snow gives a feeling of tranquility far from the maddening crowd. Here and there the shakunage rhododendron, Japanese andromeda, and putchock are beautiful when in bloom.

◆Visitor's fee: ¥600. Inclusive of copying by oneself (by tracing) the Chinese characters for a short Buddhist scripture. Open: 8:30~16:30

21. Renge-ji

This Tendai school temple was erected by Imae Chikayoshi. Near the *crane island* stonework is a rock standing erect in the pond depicting Mt. Horai. On the *tortoise island* surrounded by trees is a memorial stone to Kinoshita Jun an. Engraved on the stone is one of his well known verses. The stone lantern in front of the *hondo* is also unique to Renge-ji.

◆Visitor's fee: ¥400.　Open: 9:00~17:00

22. Shūgaku-in Imperial Villa

The photograph is of the garden at Kami no Chaya (Upper Area). The grounds are actually divided into three areas: Kami no Chaya, Naka no Chaya (Middle Area), and Shimo no Chaya (Lower Area). The Shimo no Chaya, located between the Kami and Naka no Chaya, consists of the *shoin* called Jugetsukan and a teahouse, Zorokuan. There is also a stone lantern, Yagura-doro, in this area which is highly treasured. In the Naka no Chaya, there is a *yarimizu*, the water being drawn from the nearby Otowa River, which meanders past the *kyakuden*.

◆ Permission is needed. Application should be made at the Imperial Household Agency. If there is room in the tour group on the day application is made, it may be possible to make application and be allowed entry on the same day. (Refer to page 62) There are no tours conducted in English.

23. Manshu-in

This temple was moved to the foot of Mt. Hiei by Ryosho, the son of Toshihito (builder of Katsura Imperial Villa). Both the stone lantern which has historical connections with Christianity and is located on the *crane island* and the owl shaped hand washing basin in front of the small *shoin* are well known.

◆Visitor's fee: ¥500.　Open: 9:00~16:30

24. Shisen-dō

This is where Ishikawa Jozan, an exiled retainer of Tokugawa Ieyasu, lived in seclusion. Through the influence of his studies of the Chinese classics, he constructed a unique Chinese style garden. A very peaceful garden, the silence is broken only by the sharp crack of the *sozu*.

◆Visitor's fee: ¥500.　Open: 9:00~17:00

25. Konpuku-ji

This temple was restored by the renowned Zen monk, Tesshu, during the Genroku period (1688~1704). The garden is on the south side of the *kyakuden* and is very simple, centering around the finely trimmed shrubbery. Bashoan, a small cottage reported to be connected to Matsuo Basho the famous haiku poet, as well as the grave of Yosano Buson, another well known haiku poet, are located here.

◆Visitor's fee: ¥300.　Open: 9:00~17:00

26. Shōden-ji

This temple is located more or less at the top of the base of Funayama, in Nishigamo. Traditionally, it has been said that the *hojo* and the *karamon*, or Chinese style gate, are a legacy from Fushimi Castle. The garden is called Shishi no Kowatashi, or Lioness Crossing With Her Cubs, because the rock formations appear like a lion who might be swimming across a river with her cubs. The *hojo* is famous for its paintings of mountains and rivers.

◆Visitor's fee: ¥300.　Open: 9:00~17:00

27. Kōetsu-ji

Taikyoan was the retirement teahouse of Hon'ami Koetsu. It is surrounded by the diagonally crossed bamboo fence which is attributed to be the work of Hon'ami himself, an artist in the late sixteenth early seventeenth centuries. The autumn bush clover is beautiful. There are several other *chaseki*, that is, tea rooms or smaller teahouses, in the garden; among them, Sanmitei is very well known. Koetsu's gravestone still stands on one side of the garden.

◆Visitor's fee: ¥300.　Open: 8:00~17:00

28. Kinkaku-ji

Awarajima is but one of the several islands that dot Kyokoike, a pond exemplifying the "Pond of the Seven Treasures" in the Pureland Buddhist Paradise. Alongside stands the Golden Pavilion, regilded in goldleaf after it was burned down by a crazed student in the 1950's. Built by the third Ashikaga Shogun, the pavilion was built in the Chinese Sung Dynasty style and is said to be the quintessence of the Kitayama Culture of that day. Sekkatei, the teahouse on the east side of the pond is attributed to Kanamori Sowa.

◆Visitor's fee: ¥400.　Open: 9:00~17:00

29. Ryōan-ji

The meaning of this garden, fronting the *hojo* with its fifteen rocks resting on waves of white sand, has been variously interpreted. Some say it depicts a mother lion and her cubs swimming across the water. Another interpretation holds that it symbolically portrays the nine mountains and eight seas surrounding the Buddhist world of Mt. Sumeru. The *wabisuke* camelia, the Ryōanji-style fence, and Kyoyo Pond are also very charming and of superb taste.

◆Visitor's fee: ¥500.　Open: 8:00~17:00

30. Ninna-ji

Emperor Uda completed construction on this temple, sometimes referred to as the Omuro Palace. At the foot of the hillside, a truly splendid waterfall has been arranged and northeast of the *tsukiyama*, stands Hitotei, the treasured teahouse of the previous Emperor, Kokaku.

◆Visitor's fee: ¥500.　Open: 9:00~16:30

31. Tōji-in

Muso Kokushi was designated as founder of this temple, built by Ashikaga Takauji, the first Ashikaga Shogun, (Muromachi period 1334~1568). Later, it came to be the family temple for the Ashikaga. In the Reikoden, there are wooden sculptures of all fifteen Shogun of the Ashikaga. The temple is famous for its flowers throughout the year, particularly uraku camellias

and kakitsubata irises.
◆Visitor's fee: ¥400.　Open: 8:00~17:00

32. Taizō-in
The photograph is of the west garden of the *hojo* at Taizō-in. This temple is one of the finest of the sub-temples in the Myoshin-ji complex. The west garden of the *hojo* was designed as a 50 *tsubo* (about 165 sq. me.) garden. It reminds one of a Kano style landscape painting. There is also a more recent but atypical *kansho-style* Zen garden with a three-tiered waterfall, Yoko-en, designed by Nakane Kinsaku.
◆Visitor's fee: ¥400.　Open: 9:00~17:00

33. Keishun-in
The photograph is of the east garden of the *hojo* at Keishun-in. This temple is a sub-temple within the Myoshin-ji complex. The *hojo* is surrounded by the Seijo, Shii, Shinnyo and other gardens. The trees, rocks and moss arranged in the garden form a unified reduction of the larger world of nature, and speak of an elegant and refined simplicity.
◆Visitor's fee: ¥400.　Open: 9:00~17:00 (open until 16:30 in winter)

34. Hōkongō-in
Among the softly undulating hills of southeastern Narabigaoka stands Hōkongō-in, traditionally said to be a temple of the Nara period Risshu school of Buddhism. Rinken, a priest from Ninna-ji, is said to have made the stroll garden centering it around Osono Pond. This garden depicts the Pureland Paradise. Among other treasures to be found here is a statue of Amida Nyorai.
◆Visitor's fee: ¥400.　Open: 9:00~16:00

35. Ōsawa Pond
Reported to be a copy of Lake Tungting in China, there is a rock in the pond called Teikoishi (located between Tenjinjima and Kikugajima). North of the pond are the remains of a waterfall called Nakoso, once a famous place in Japanese poetry. Around mid-autumn a boat takes one out on the pond in the evening for moon-viewing.
◆Visitor's fee: No fee required to stroll around the pond, but

there is a ¥500 fee to go in to see Daikakuji.　Open: 9:00~16:30

36. Giō-ji
The remnants of Ojo-in, depicted in the Heian period classic, Tales of Heike, was reconstructed during the Meiji period. There are statues enshrined to Taira Kiyomori, Hotoke Gozen, Gio and her mother inside the very modest thatch roofed *hondo* or sanctuary.
◆Visitor's fee: ¥300.　Open: 9:00~16:45

37. Tenryū-ji
Ashikaga Takauji built this temple in memory of Emperor Godaigo, with Muso Kokushi designated as founder. It is delightful to stroll around the *tsukiyama* and *chitei* and to take in the greater and lesser *hojo* with the Arashiyama and Mt. Atago as a backdrop.
◆Visitor's fee: ¥500.　Open: 8:30~17:00

38. Rokuō-in
Between the Sanmon and Chumon gates, there extends a simple stone pathway surrounded by sugar maples. The pathway takes the shape of the Japanese hiragana character "く". From the *kyakuden* the view of the emerald moss fronting the *shariden*, a sort of burial hall, with the Arashiyama as a backdrop, is simple but impressive.
◆Visitor's fee: ¥300.　Open: 9:00~17:00

39. Umenomiya Taisha (Shrine)
A god whom sake makers are said to revere is enshrined here. In the spring, there are 150 yaezakura (a type of multi-petaled cherry tree) reflecting their images in the pond. With the coming of summer, the pond abounds with the bright colorful clusters of blue flag irises in bloom.
◆ Visitor's fee: ¥400 (though walking through the grounds inself is free)　Open: 9:00~17:00

40. Jizō-in
Embraced by the bamboo groves of the Nishiyama or Western Hills, Jizō-in is often referred to as the "Bamboo Temple." Upon entering the gate, the path approaching the temple itself,

conveying a feeling of calmness and tranquility, runs directly through the groves of bamboo; the stone walkway leading to the *hojo* feels refreshingly cool in the early morning.
◆Visitor's fee: ¥500.　Open: 9:00~16:40

41. Katsura Imperial Villa

The photograph is of the Shokintei Garden at Katsura Imperial Villa. Prince Toshihito, well versed in Classical Japanese and Chinese literature, built the estate at Katsura over a period of several years beginning in the early 1600's. The pond garden centers around a pond that takes the shape of the Chinese character for heart or mind. The several elaborately designed and constructed teahouses, among them Sanshoin, Gepparo, and Shokintei, have all been done in exquisite and refined taste and perfect harmony.
◆Permission is needed. Application should be made at the Imperial Household Agency. If there is room in the tour group on the day application is made, it may be possible to make application and be allowed entry on the same day. (Refer to page 62) There are no tours conducted in English.

42. Byōdō-in

The chief advisor to the emperor, Fujiwara Yorimichi (922 ~1074) built the Phoenix Hall as an extension to his father's villa. Byōdō-in became a temple in 1052. The statue of Amida Nyorai sculpted by Jocho is enshrined in the Phoenix Hall. The reflection mirrored in the pond is especially lovely when the wisteria are in bloom in late spring.
◆Visitor's fee: ¥600.　Open: 9:00~17:00

43. Kajū-ji

Emperor Daigo founded the temple which now has more than a thousand years of history behind it. Utilizing the surrounding hills as *borrowed scenery*, the garden area opens out around Himuro Pond. It is also famous for its 750 year old juniper tree as well as its *gagyuseki*, a natural stone in the shape of a cow at rest.
◆Visitor's fee: ¥400.　Open: 9:00~16:00

44. Zuishin-in

This is the temple of the famous Heian period poetess, Onono Komachi. The brilliant green moss covers the whole garden earning it the name Moss Temple of Rakuson (southeast Kyoto). Behind the *hondo*, there is a traditional three-tiered waterfall, while the view in front of the *shoin* gives a feeling of spaciousness.
◆Visitor's fee: ¥400.　Open: 9:00~16:30

45. Jōnan-gū(Shrine)

The photograph is of the Rakusuien Garden at Jōnan-gū Shrine. The garden was constructed after the Second World War by Nakane Kinsaku, reviving elements from the earlier Heian, Muromachi, and Momoyama period gardens. There is also a dry landscape garden, Rikyu no Niwa. It is famous for its benishi-daresakura or drooping cherry trees, azaleas, and wisteria.
◆Visitor's fee: ¥400.　Open: 9:00~16:00

46. Shūon-an

This temple is sometimes called Ikkyu-ji, because of its historical ties to Sojun Ikkyu Zenji, a famous Zen priest. The garden area folds around three sides of the *hojo*. The garden to the rear of the *hojo* is the main one, and extends to the mausoleum built for Ikkyu. There is also a garden called Kokyu no Niwa designed to fit in well with the tea ceremony.
◆Visitor's fee: ¥400.　Open: 9:00~16:30

47. Jōruri-ji

This temple is located in the southern extremity of Yamashiro, in Kamocho. The garden centers around a pond and is representative of those gardens depicting the Pure Land or Western Paradise. This one was constructed during the Heian period. On the opposite shore of the garden there is a small hill upon which stands a three-tiered pagoda with a statue of Yakushi Nyorai (the Saint of Healing) enshrined inside. The stone-works functioning to protect. the shore and the delicate curves of the shore itself are exquisite.
○Entry to the grounds is free (¥300 for the Main Hall).
◆Open: 9:00~17:00 (10:00~16:30, Dec.-Feb.)

■ Garden and Other Terms

●Ajijke pond

A pond constructed in the shape of the first letter of the Sanskrit alphabet.

●Bugyo

A high ranking administrative official appointed by the emperor during the Heian period and by the shogun in later periods to perform certain specified tasks. As a *bugyo*, Kobori Enshu worked as a master gardener.

●Chitei

The shore of a pond.

●Chisenshiki teien

A pond garden, sometimes including a waterfall or island. There are three basic types; *shuyushiki*, a garden viewed from a boat rowed around the pond, *kaiyushiki*, a garden viewed from several vantage points while walking or strolling along the path through the garden, and, *kanshoshiki*, a pond or dry landscape garden viewed from inside a room, perhaps from inside the *shoin* or *hojo*.

●Fusuma

The sliding doors which separate rooms and are often covered with heavy paper or cloth. In many cases, calligraphy or pictures are painted on them.

●Gogan

A rock formation functioning as a protective or maintenance barrier for a pond or stream.

●Hiraniwa

A type of garden which is basically flat without any pond or *tsukiyama* type mounds or hills.

●Hojo

The abbot's quarters. The size of the *hojo* varies widely with the prestige and prosperity of the temple. A *hojo* was originally a small room or hut of about 10 feet square.

●Hondo

The temple sanctuary housing a statue of Buddha, e.g., Sha-kyamuni or Amida Buddha. The *hondo* is also where various Buddhist ceremonies are performed.

●Horai teien

A type of garden depicting the mythical Mt. Horai where many religious sages are said to gather for religious practices and training. In garden design, this motif is sometimes referred to as Horaijima, or Horai Island, implying that the mountain rises out of the great sea as an island.

●Ichimatsu moyo

A checkered pattern used tastefully at Tōfuku-ji.

●Ishiniwa

A garden employing rock as a base along with white sand or moss to create a particular affect.

●Iwagumi

A rock or group of rocks used to represent waterfalls, islands, and mountains. *Iwagumi* comprise the basic medium for Japanese gardens.

●Izumidono

A technique employed in garden construction whereby the edge of the pond extends directly up to or even under the edge of the building from which it is viewed, in order to induce a feeling of the building having been built over water.

●Jodoshiki teien

A garden depicting the Pureland Paradise. Byōdō-in and Jōruri-ji are famous examples with their pond gardens in front of the Amida Hall.

●Kaisando

A building in which the ashes of the founder of a temple are enshrined.

●Kamejima

An element in pond gardens depicting Mt. Horai. Sometimes a central element in the dry landscape gardens. Comprised of one or occasionally several rocks. Literally, *kamejima* means tortoise island.

●Kareike

A garden which does not employ water as an element in its composition. One type of dry landscape garden. Literally, *kareike* means dry pond.

●Karesansui teien

A dry landscape garden which utilizes white sand, rocks, or moss to symbolize ponds, seas, or oceans. This style garden developed during the Momoyama period with the influence of Zen when simplicity was of the essence.

●Karikomi

Trees, bushes, or shrubs clipped to a prescribed shape and employed to depict scenery. They often represent distant mountains or islands out in the seas or oceans.

●Koetsugaki/(Gagyugaki)

An unique style of bamboo fence designed by Hon'ami Koetsu.

●Kyakuden

A reception room or sometimes a building used for receiving or entertaining guests.

●Nobedan

A paved stone path comprised of flat stones laid out at the approach to or around a garden. Its purpose is both functional and aesthetic.

●Roji

Literally, meaning "dewy path," it is sometimes referred to as a tea garden. The *roji* includes the path and the garden leading to the teahouse.

●Ryumonseki

A rock placed at the head of a waterfall, reminiscent of the Ryumon, a waterfall in the upper reaches of the Yellow River in China.

●Samon

The white sand or gravel found in dry landscape gardens and raked to form various patterns of waves.

●Sanson iwa

Based on the Buddhist concept of a trinity, the central rock is the largest of the "three holy rocks," and is flanked by two smaller attendant rocks. Amida Buddha surrounded by Kannon and Seishi Bodhisattvas is one type; Shakyamuni Buddha attended by two saints, or Yakushi Nyorai flanked by Nikko and Gakko Bodhisattvas are two others. That is, the same concept is expressed slightly differently depending upon the Buddhist school.

●Sawatari

Flat rocks arranged to cross a pond or stream.

●Shakkei

Natural scenery which is not an actual part of the garden, but rather borrowed to enhance the feeling of spaciousness of the garden. Mt. Hiei behind Entsu-ji and Arashiyama behind Tenryū-ji are well known examples.

●Shinden zukuri

A style of palace architecture prominent during the apex of the influence of the Fujiwara family during the Heian period, and which set the standard in architecture for the nobility and upper class in later periods.

●Shin gyo so

In the tea ceremony, a concept implying formal, semi-formal, and informal. Later, the idea was utilized in designing garden paths. The *shin* style uses cut stones only, *gyo* style stone paths are a combination of cut and natural stones, while *so* stone paths use natural stones only.

●Shoin

Originally, the *shoin* was a large room or hall used by the monks for study. Later, it came to be used as a room or building for special guests. *Shoin zukuri*, or *shoin* style architecture was employed largely by the samurai class.

●Shukukeishiki teien

Miniaturized scenery. A portion of a garden imitating some famous scenic spot on a reduced scale. An example of this is the miniaturized version of Ama no Hashidate in front of Shokintei at the Katsura Villa.

●Shumisenshiki teien

According to Buddhist cosmology, *shumisen*, or Mt. Sumeru soars above all others in the center of this world, and is surrounded by nine mountains and eight seas.

●Sozu

A device made of bamboo intended to frighten away deer. Water, trickling into and eventually filling a section of bamboo, causes a shift in the balance. All the water suddenly pours out and the bamboo, now being empty, returns to its original position. In doing so, it makes a loud cracking sound as it strikes the rock upon which it was resting. Again, water trickles into the mouth of the bamboo and the process is repeated.

●Tobiishi

Stepping stones laid as a path in a garden for the purpose of protecting the moss, or in a pond used for crossing in place of a bridge.

●Tsuboniwa

A small inner garden surrounded on all sides.

●Tsukiyama

The building up of sand or rocks to form a mound which in turn represents a mountain.

● Tsukubai

A hand washing basin, usually made of stone, placed along the path leading to a teahouse.

● Tsurushima

A crane island. One element in a Horai style garden; usually the vertical rock partner to the *kameshima* or tortoise island, which is laid horizontally. The *tsurushima* motif is usually comprised of one or two rocks.

● Yakuishi

Rocks placed either in *shoin* or tea gardens for a particular function.

● Yarimizu

A narrow stream flowing through a garden.

■ Historical Periods and Prominent Garden Styles

Heian Period (794~1185)

Large pond gardens to match *shinden zukuri*, or palace style architecture. Viewed either while strolling or by boat.

Kamakura Period (1185~1333)

Pond gardens for strolling through, employing more rocks and stones.

Nanbokucho Period (1336~1392)

Southern Northern dynasties period. Dry landscape gardens.

Muromachi Period (1334~1568)

Zen influenced dry landscape gardens and large pond gardens.

Momoyama Period (1568~1603)

Castle building period when garden design incorporated massive rocks and stonework.

Tokugawa period or Edo Period (1603~1868)

Synthesis of pond gardens and *roji*.

Meiji period (1868~1912)

Inovation in garden design.

Taisho period (1912~1926)

Showa period (1926~1989)

Heisei period (1989~　　)

■ Application to see the Kyoto Imperial Palaces and Villas

● Kyoto Imperial Palace

Permission is needed. There is no age limit, but children should be accompanied by an adult (20 years of age or over). Groups must be smaller than nine persons per tour (Larger groups have separate tour times and must apply for permission in a different way).

Tour times; 10:00a.m. and 2:00p.m. Apply for permission in advance (at least 20 minutes before the tour time) at the Office.

● Sentō Imperial Palace
● Katsura Imperial Villa
● Shūgaku-in Imperial Villa

Permission is needed. Only adults 20 years of age or older are allowed. Groups must be smaller than 4 per tour.

Tour Times:

＊Sentō Imperial Palace   11:00a.m. and 1:30p.m.

＊Katsura Imperial Villa   10:00a.m. and 2:00p.m.

＊Shūgaku-in Imperial Villa   9:00a.m. 10:00a.m. 11:00a.m. 1:30p.m. and 3:00p.m.

For a reply please send two copies of the applications form and a self-addressed envelope with sufficient postage to the: Director Imperial Household Agency, Kyoto Office, 3 Kyoto-Gyoen, Kamigyo-ku, Kyoto 602-0881 JAPAN, at least one to three months before your visit. Or, make a reservation by phone (Only Japanese is spoken). As spring and fall are the busiest seasons, please reserve well in advance.

＊Telephone number: (075)211-1215.

＊Open weekdays and Saturdays in April, May, October, November and the third Saturday of every month. Closed on all other Saturdays, Sundays, national holidays, Dec. 25th-Jan. 5th and the days of ceremonies.

☐ Infomation

To enjoy your limited vacation time in Kyoto, it's a good idea to visit the Tourist Information Center just across and up the street (Karasuma Dori, west side) from Kyoto Station's Central Exit. There is a Japanese staff who will be most helpful-and, in English. The Information Center will provide, free of charge, detailed information on transportation, lodging, meals, sightseeing, etc. In addition, the staff will be most helpful in answering any questions you might have regarding such diverse topics as traditional crafts and local products, history, or local church services. The Center also has a supply of introductory pamphlets on other cities and areas of Japan.

●Tourist Information Center, Kyoto Office
Kyoto Tower Bldg., 1st Floor, Shichijo Karasuma-sagaru, Kyoto.
Tel: 075(371)5649 Hours: 9:00-5:00 Closed Saturday afternoons, Sundays and National holidays.
Free telephone service: When calling from outside Kyoto, between 9:00a.m.~5:00p.m., please call the following toll-free number for information on events in Kansai: 0120-444-800.
This free service is available every day of the year. For information on events in Tokyo, call: 0120-222-800.

When traveling within Kyoto City by the Municipal Bus (in Japanese, shiei bus) or Municipal Subway lines, the "One-day pass" is most economical. One adult pass for ¥1,200 entitles the user to unlimited boarding privileges for the local bus and subway, as well as the Kyoto Bus Line (a private company). For most destinations in the city, the bus fare is ¥220, the subway, ¥200-¥270. The MK Taxi service is convenient for the foreign tourist as there are a number of drivers quite fluent in English. Tel: 075(721)2237.

☐ Mini Japanese Language Lesson

●-ji or -dera (tera) means temple. For example, Daitoku-ji, Sesshudera.
●-in or -an usually indicate a sub-temple within a larger temple complex. For example, Konchi-in within the Nanzen-ji complex or Daisen-in within the Daitoku-ji complex.
●-miya, -gū, and taisha indicate Shinto shrines of varying ranks. For example, Heian Jingū and Umenomiya Taisha are rather large Shinto shrines of fairly high rank.
●-cho and -machi are the equivalent to a neighborhood.
●-ku is a somewhat larger geographical area equivalent to a ward or burrough. For example, Kyoto's Sakyo-ku extends far beyond the city proper. A bus trip to Sanzen-in will take you quite a way into the countryside.
●-michi and -dori are the equivalents of street and avenue or boulevard, respectively. Jingu Michi runs north and south in front of Heian Jingū, Kawaramachi Dori is one of the main north-south avenues running through what is now the main commercial district of Kyoto.

○All words or expressions in italix will be found in the section on Garden and Other Terms on pages 60~62.
○All Japanese names are listed in the Japanese order with the family name listed first, followed by the first name. For example, Tokugawa and Kobori are family names while Ieyasu and Enshu are their first names.